HTML Programming for Beginners

How to Learn HTML in Less Than One Week. The Ultimate Step-by-Step Complete Course from Novice to Advance Programmer

William Brown

Table of contents

INTRODUCTION..5

CHAPTER 1: WHAT IS HTML..7

1.1: Introduction to the Web...7

1.2: What is Web Development..9

1.3: Front-End Programming Languages.................................11

1.4: Introduction to HTML..14

1.5: Advantages and Disadvantages of HTML........................17

CHAPTER 2: HOW HTML WORKS...19

2.1: HTML Editors..19

2.2: Basic Page Structure...21

2.3: HTML Elements...26

2.4: HTML Attributes..36

2.5: Charsets...46

CHAPTER 3: BASIC RULES AND PRACTICAL APPLICATIONS.......48

3.1: Semantic Elements...48

3.2: HTML Links...58

3.3: HTML Forms..62

3.4: CSS along with HTML..73

3.5: Responsive Web Design..78

CHAPTER 4: MAKE YOUR OWN HTML PROGRAM.......................83

CHAPTER 5: MISTAKES TO AVOID IN HTML..............................121

5.1: Basic Syntax and Implementation Errors........................121

CONCLUSION..126

Introduction

Welcoming you to a new learning experience and a step-by-step guide on coding web pages and web designing is an accessible yet creative and responsive website. It doesn't matter if you have a programming background or learning from scratch; this book will cover all the essential topics that will help you grasp the concepts of HTML front-end development. Throughout the book, various basic features of HTML, elements, attributes, and tags will be used with other concepts and guide you on how to make your own HTML program and what mistakes to avoid while doing so.

There is no right or wrong when reading this book; it depends on the reader and how they outcome from it. The book strategy also ensures that there is enough motivation and devotion to the learners by taking challenges after each subject to help refresh readers' experience and make them believe that they can now take upon any challenge. Hope you have an excellent and practical learning experience with this book, and upon completion, you've mastered the beginner-level HTML and how to implement it in various areas. It is indeed an exciting and enjoyable book to read while you're either finding a new part-time hobby or for educational purposes. The goal is to stay persistent and keen while practicing. Wishing you great luck with the journey ahead!

Chapter 1: What is HTML

1.1: Introduction to the Web

The World Wide Web is an interactive form of public web pages that can be accessed through the Internet. The Web is not the same as the Internet; it is one of many applications that run in its background.

Tim Berners-Lee introduced the architecture of the World Wide Web. In 1990, at the CERN physics research lab, he developed the first database server, web browser, and webpage on his computer. He revealed his existence on the alt. hypertext newsgroup in 1991, marking the first official release on the Web. Two types of computers are connected to the Internet:

1. Servers

2. Clients

Websites are information saved on servers that are computers that host (or store files for) websites. Servers are connected to a vast network of information known as the internet or the World Wide Web. Browsers such as Google, Firefox, and Internet Explorer, are computer programs that load websites through the internet connection. The client is another term for your machine.

To access a website from the web, an IP address is required for each computer. A string of unique numbers known as IP address is assigned for each device connected to the Internet. To separate billions of websites and computers connecting to the internet, each user has an IP address. Although an IP address may be used to access a website, most internet users tend to use domain names or search engines.

The HyperText Transfer Protocol (HTTP) establishes a connection between you and your website request and the remote server that stores all website data. It is a set of rules that administers how messages are transmitted over the internet. It enables you to navigate through different site pages and websites.

When a website is searched on a search engine, HTTP offers a mechanism that allows the client (computer) and server to communicate in the same language when sending and receiving requests and replies over the internet. It acts as an interpreter between you and the internet, reading your website submission, reading the code returned from the server, and translating it into a website for you.

Writing code for servers and databases using programming languages is referred to as coding. The term "language" refers to a collection of vocabulary and grammatical rules for interacting with computers. Special instructions, abbreviations, and punctuation that computers and programs can only interpret are also included. At least one coding language is used to create all applications, but languages differ by platform, operating system, and design. Different programming languages exist for coding websites which are divided into two groups: front-end and backend.

1.2: What is Web Development

The process of creating a website is known as Web Development. It could refer to anything from a simple plain-text website to a complicated web application or social network growth. Web development has become a growing industry since the commercialization of the Internet. Businesses who want to use their website for advertising and selling goods and services to consumers are increasing this sector's growth.

Developers have been investing in more creative and immersive Web pages thanks to an ever-growing range of software and technology. Furthermore, Web developers are also assisting with software delivery that was formerly only available as desktop applications as Web services. It has created many ways for information and media distribution to be decentralized.

Web development expertise is in high demand and well-compensated worldwide, making it an excellent career choice. It is one of the most readily available higher-paying sectors since it does not require a conventional university degree.

The internet will not be phased out anytime soon. It has evolved into the world's primary portal for science, communication, education, and entertainment. There are 4.2 billion internet subscribers worldwide as of 2019. That is more than half of the world's people, and they use the internet for a wide range of purposes.

What is the one thing that all these factors have in common? They need a website, and each website necessitates the services of an experienced web developer. Web production is a quickly growing sector as well. According to recent surveys, Web developer jobs are projected to increase by 13% between now and 2028. That is a lot quicker than any other engineering job.

Many people learn web coding to build websites for themselves or find work in the industry. However, since it is easy to get started, it is also an excellent option if you only want a general introduction to coding. Some claim that it is the most straightforward kind of coding to learn for beginners. It is simple to set up, produces immediate results, and there is plenty of online instruction.

Web architecture is divided into front-end development (also known as client-side development) and backend development (also called server-side development). Front-end development is the process of designing the text, interface, and interaction that a user perceives when they open a web application. HTML, CSS, and JavaScript are used to do this. Backend production oversees what happens behind the scenes of a website. A database is sometimes utilized to create front-end page. Backend scripts can be written in various programming languages and systems, including PHP, Java, ASP.NET.

Learning to code is a rewarding experience, but it can also be challenging and stressful. A motivation to create, a problem-solving mind, and perseverance in the face of setbacks are the most valuable assets you can have as you study further.

1.3: Front-End Programming Languages

Client-side development, also considered to be front-end development, is a relatively unknown Internet specialization. People working in this field have been called by various names in the past, including web designer, coder, front-ender, etc. But its core roles have remained the same though evolving with the

Internet's advancement. It is a pivotal position that necessitates artistic sensitivity as well as programmatic rigors.

What began as HTML, JavaScript, and CSS have evolved significantly over the past 20 years. HTML5 architecture has surpassed Flash development in popularity. The diverse and interactive internet we use regularly is a credit to front-end architecture and front-end programming languages.

Any step performed by a Front-End developer assures a positive user experience. All of the tidy flourishes and seamless page launches are the responsibility of a Front-End developer. If a developer may be concerned with a site's aesthetics, their primary concern is its efficiency. Since they collaborate with web designers and backend developers, front-end developers must be both imaginative and technical.

Front-end languages include:

- HTML, newer versions such as HTML5 as well

- CSS – Cascading Style Sheets

- JavaScript

- WebAssembly

These languages are considered the backbone of Front-end programming and have kept on evolving. It is important to note that HTML and CSS are not programming languages. CSS is a styling language, and HTML is a markup language. However, JavaScript is a programming language. As a result, they are all web languages, but they have various purposes. The three languages are relatively simple to pick up and have a great deal of versatility and innovation. These three languages and JavaScript frameworks are needed for being a good Front End developer.

The foundation of every website development process is HyperText Markup Language (HTML), without which a web page would not exist. Hypertext refers to text that contains links, also known as hyperlinks. When a person clicks on a hyperlinked word or sentence, it takes them to another web page.

CSS (Cascading Style Sheets) is a programming language that manages a website's appearance and helps it get its distinct look. It is accomplished by retaining style sheets that rest on top of other style guidelines caused by other factors such as computer screen size and resolution. Whereas JavaScript is an incident-based imperative programming code (in contrast to HTML's declaratory language prototype) that can be used to convert a stationary HTML page into a dynamic Graphical User Interface.

The web's purpose has primarily been about sharing information since its creation, but this data-driven movement risks drowning people in a sea of isolated, random information factoids that few can comprehend and far less interested in. A front-end developer's mission is to build a simple, straightforward, and quick web page-based interface for the websites that help people understand and care about knowledge by placing it in context, exposing its validity, and revealing their unspoken or explicit interconnection.

1.4: Introduction to HTML

HTML (HyperText Markup Language) is a mark-up language which specifies how the content is organized. It is divided into two parts: HyperText, which provides links to other texts, and Markup, which defines the basic form and presentation of raw text.

HTML is made up of a collection of elements that you can use to wrap various portions of the subject to get it to look or behave a certain way. The encircling tags may be used to render a word or picture hyperlink to another place, italicize words, change the font size, and so on.

HTML is not a programming language, so it cannot do anything like build complex functionality. Instead, it allows you to arrange and type documents in the same way as Microsoft Word does.

HTML has become an official web format because of its rapid growth in popularity. The World Wide Web of Consortium oversees maintaining and developing HTML standards.

Tim Berners-Lee, a scientist at the CERN research institute in Switzerland, introduced HTML. Tim developed a concept of a hypertext structure built on the Internet. In 1991, he released the first version of HTML, which consisted of 18 HTML tags. Since then, additional tags and attributes (tag modifiers) have been added to the markup for each new iteration of the HTML language.

The new status of the language can be seen on the W3C website at any time. The launch of HTML5 in 2014 was the most significant update to the language. It added up numerous innovative semantic tags to the markup, such as <article>, <header>, and <footer>, that show the context of their type.

HTML is entirely text-based; it can be edited by simply opening it in a text editor like Notepad++, Visual Studio Code, or Emacs. Any HTML text editor can be used to create or update an HTML file, and any web browser, such as Chrome or Firefox, can view the file as a webpage, whether it is called with an.html file extension.

The use of a document type declaration at the start of the text file is perhaps the most basic HTML conventions. Since it is the piece that unambiguously reminds a machine that this is an HTML file, it often appears first in the text. Usually, the text header looks like this:!DOCTYPE html>. It should all be written in this format, with no content or breaks in between. A machine would not accept any material before this declaration as HTML.

Another essential factor for making an HTML file is that it be saved with the.html extension. The file extension signals HTML to the machine from the outside of the file, while the doctype statement signals HTML from the inside of the file. A device can indicate whether it is reading an HTML file or not. When uploading files to the site, it is imperative since the webserver must know what to do with the files before sending them to a client computer to read the contents.

A user can use any of the other syntactic resources of HTML to modify a web page after writing the doctype and storing it as an HTML file. When they are finished, they will most certainly have multiple HTML files relating to different website sites. Since each page references the individual file paths of the other pages, allowing connections between them, the user must upload these files in the same hierarchy that they stored them in. Since the listed file paths do not fit the pages, uploading them in a different order will cause links to split and pages to be lost.

For those who want to work as a Software Developer, particularly in the Web Development field, you will need to learn HTML because you cannot create a website without it. HTML is the fundamental requirement for a developer to understand when designing a website from the bottom up.

- **Learn HTML**: Learning HTML is the first step in learning Web Development. If you have mastered HTML, you will be able to quickly create plain, static websites.

- **Can work as a freelancer**: Since web production offers the most opportunities for freelancing, learning HTML will undoubtedly assist you in obtaining the best website development deals available.

1.5: Advantages and Disadvantages of HTML

To start, any web developer or web designer must learn HTML. HTML5 is the most recent edition of HTML, and it is exceptionally modern and robust. HTML has many setbacks and drawbacks.

Pros:

- A commonly used language with a large community and a wealth of resources.

- Every web browser supports it natively.

- It has a simple learning curve.

- It is entirely free and open source.

- Markup that is neat and reliable.

- The World Wide Web Consortium oversees maintaining official web specifications (W3C).

- Backend development languages such as PHP and Python are easily integrated.

- Audio, video, and images, among other things, can be easily embedded.

Cons:

- It prevents the user from implementing logic. Therefore, even though they use the same elements, such as headers and footers, each web page must

be generated separately.

- Some browsers are reluctant to implement new features.

- Browser behavior can be unpredictable (for example, older browsers do not always make newer tags).

- It is tricky to build interactive websites.

- Each page has a different coding page.

- It has many security compromises on its own and needs other programming languages to support the website's security.

Chapter 2: How HTML works

2.1: HTML Editors

It is an application that allows you to edit HTML, which is the markup of any web page. While any text editor can manage the HTML markup on a web page, dedicated HTML editors can provide more ease and flexibility. Many HTML editors, for example, support HTML and similar technology like XML, CSS, and ECMAScript or JavaScript.

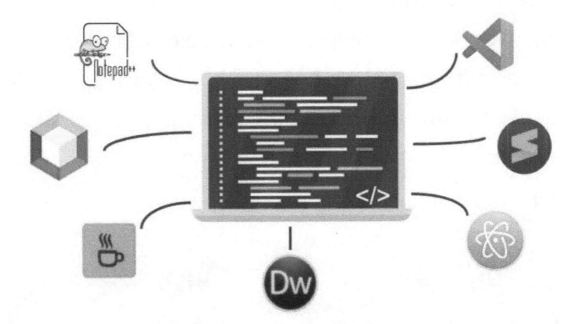

Professional HTML editors can be used to build and modify web pages. However, a basic text editor such as Notepad (PC) or TextEdit (Mac) is recommended for studying HTML (Mac). Developers believe that learning HTML is best accomplished by using a basic text editor.

Version control, validation, and link-checking, code cleaning and structuring, uploading by FTP or WebDAV, spell-checking, and project structuring are all features that text editors widely used for HTML provide either built-in functionality or interaction with external software. A Few functions, like link testing or validation, can rely on online resources, which necessitate a network link.

This book will be using Visual Studio Code as it has 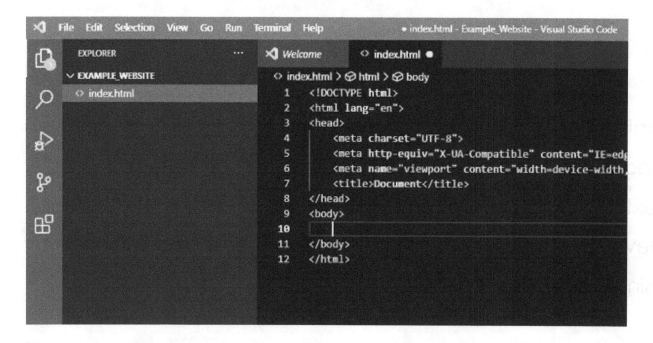 an easy user interface and provides an easy command prompt. It comes with simple HTML programming assistance out of the box. Syntax highlighting, IntelliSense intelligent completions, and custom formatting are all available. VS Code also has excellent Emmet support.

Here is how the programming prompt looks like:

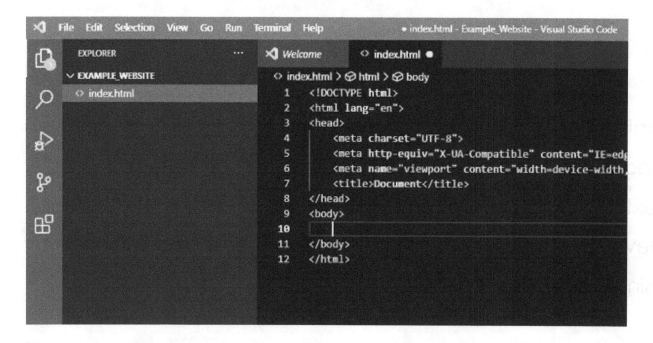

2.2: Basic Page Structure

In this section, the basic structure of an HTML page and how different components are used will be explained briefly. It incorporates the fundamental building blocks that all web pages are built on.

Tags (and their attributes), character-based data types, character references, and entity references are only a few of the core components of HTML markup. Most HTML tags are paired, such as <h1> and </h1>, but others, such as <img>, represent empty elements and are therefore unpaired. The start tag is the first of a pair of tags, and the end tag is the second (they are also called opening tags and closing tags). The HTML document type declaration, which enables standards mode encoding, is another important element.

Elements and Tags:

An HTML element is one of several types of HTML nodes that make up an HTML document component. HTML documents are made up of a hierarchy of primary HTML nodes, such as text nodes and HTML elements, giving the document semantics and formatting (e.g., making text bold, organizing it into paragraphs, lists, and tables, or embed hyperlinks and images). HTML attributes can be defined for each variable.

```
<> index.html > ⬡ html > ⬡ body
  1   <!DOCTYPE html>
  2   <html>
  3   <head>
  4
  5   </head>
  6   <body>
  7
  8   </body>
  9   </html>
```

Document structure elements:

The main structure of an HTML document contains a document type declaration, <html> tag, <head>, and <body> tags.

<!DOCTYPE html>:

A document type declaration must appear at the top of any HTML document: <!DOCTYPE html>. It is not technically a tag but the essential declaration at the start of an HTML document and must appear once at the start. It specifies that a document is in an HTML format. There is no case difference in the doctype declaration.

<html> Tag:

It is an HTML document's root feature, which contains all other components. The HTML element separates the beginning and end of an HTML document.

<head> Tag:

A webpage's "behind the scenes" features are included in the head tag. At the front end of a website, elements in the head are not visible on the browser. An HTML document's information and metadata are processed in this container. It contains a few tags defined below:

1. **<base> Tag:**

For all relative links and other connections in the text, specifies a base URL. Any aspect that corresponds to an external resource must appear before it. Each document can only have one base> element in HTML.

Syntax: <base href="any URL">

```
<> index.html > ...
 1    <!DOCTYPE html>
 2    <html>
 3    <head>
 4        <base href="https://www.google.com/" target="_blank">
 5        <link rel="stylesheet" type="text/css" href="styles.css">
 6    </head>
 7    <body>
 8
 9    </body>
10    </html>
11
```

2. **<link> Tag:**

The link tag defines a link between a document and an external resource. To link to external style sheets, use the link suffix. This aspect can be repeated, but it only appears in the head segment. Only attributes are present in the link element; otherwise, it is empty.

Syntax: <link rel="stylesheet" type="css" href="styles.css">

3. <meta> Tag:

The term "metadata" refers to data-related material. In HTML, the meta> tag contains information about an HTML script, or, to put it another way, it provides crucial information about a document. These tags are used to add name/value pairs to HTML documents that define properties such as the expiration date, author name, list of keywords, document author, and so on.

Syntax: <meta attribute-name="data">

Some <meta> attributes are listed below:

name	This Attribute is used to specify the property's name. **Syntax:** <meta name="value">
http-equiv	The HTTP response message header is obtained using this Attribute. The "refresh" is the default http-equiv type. **Syntax:** <meta http-equiv="content-type"/>

content	This Attribute is used to specify the value of a property.
	Syntax: <meta content="data">
charset	An HTML file's character encoding is defined using this Attribute.
	Syntax: <meta charset="character-set">

```
<head>
    <meta name="attributes" charset="UTF-8" content="Meta Tags, Metadata"/>
    <meta http-equiv="refresh" content="8" />
    <title>HTML</title>
</head>
```

4. <title> Tag:

In HTML, the title tag is used to specify the document's title. It changes the title in the toolbar of the browser. In the search engine results, it shows the page's title.

Syntax: <title> webpage title </title>

<body> Tag:

The body tag is used to enclose all a webpage's identifiable text. In other words, the body material is what appears on the front end of the browser.

Syntax: <body> other nested tags </body>

The primary <head> tags do not display anything on the webpage. It simply demonstrates the basic pattern for writing HTML code and names the page's title.

2.3: HTML Elements

We will go into all the fundamentals of HTML coding. When we first begin coding in HTML, we must consider and add several tags. These tags assist with element organizing and simple formatting in our script or web pages. These step-by-step instructions will walk you through the HTML creation process.

Case Sensitive:

HTML is not case sensitive. You can use lowercase or uppercase letters, <HTML> and <html> are the same thing. Either one or the other can be used for accuracy. It is best to avoid mixing and matching and code in a specific order to avoid any errors. This book will use all lowercase HTML commands.

```
<> index.html > ⊗ html > ⊗ body
1   <!DOCTYPE html>
2   <html>
3   <head>
4
5   </head>
6   <body>
7
8   </body>
9   </html>
```

Nested Elements:

HTML elements can be nested, which means they can be stacked on top of each other (this means that elements can contain other elements). All HTML documents consist of nested HTML elements.

HTML Comments:

In HTML code, the comment attribute (<!-- Comment -->) is used to insert comments. It is a safe coding technique so that both the coder and the reader can comprehend the text. It is beneficial to comprehend the complicated code. The comment tag comes in handy when debugging code.

- It is an essential piece of code that is swept off (ignored) by web browsers, i.e., the browser does not view it.

- It aids the coder and reader in comprehending the code in question, especially in complex source code.

Syntax: <!-- Any text written as comments -->

Container and Empty tags:

Tags are divided into two categories: container and empty. The container tag wraps text or graphics around itself and comes in a pair with an opening and a

```
<html>

  <body><!--the open tag-->

   <p>Open and close tags</p>

   </body><!--the close tag-->

</html>
```

On the closing tag, note the forward-slash (/). It then informs the browser that the label is no longer active.

The empty tag, on the other hand, stands alone. The <br> tag is used to introduce a line break. These tags do not need to be wrapped around content, and they do not need to be closed.

HTML Headings:

These tags assist us in giving headings to a webpage's text. Most of these codes are written inside the body tag. From h1> to h6>, HTML provides us with six heading codes. The heading is shown in a different style and font size for each name.

- Search engines use headings to catalog the form and content of a website.

- Relevant subjects are highlighted with headings.

- They offer useful information and educate us about the document's layout.

```html
<!DOCTYPE html>

<html>

  <head>

    <title>Learning HTML</title>

  </head>

  <body>

    <h1>Heading 1</h1> <!--This tag is used for heading size 1-->

    <h2>Heading 2</h2> <!--This tag is used for heading size 2-->

    <h3>Heading 3</h3> <!--This tag is used for heading size 3-->

    <h4>Heading 4</h4> <!--This tag is used for heading size 4-->

    <h5>Heading 5</h5> <!--This tag is used for heading size 5-->

    <h6>Heading 6</h6> <!--This tag is used for heading size 6-->

  </body>

</html>
```

Here is how the browser text would look like, shown in the image.

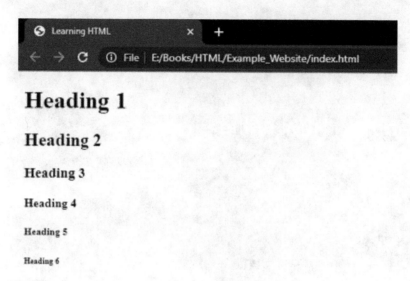

The page's title is displayed in the browser window, and the text entered with different heading tags varies in size gradually.

HTML Paragraphs:

These tags assist in the creation of paragraph statements on a website. They begin with a <p> tag and end with a </p> tag. The <br> tag is used to sever the line, which serves as a carriage return. It is an empty tag.

- As previously stated, the p>tag immediately adds space before and after any paragraph, which is essentially browser margins.

- When a user inserts several spaces, the browser compresses them into one.

- When a user inserts several lines, the browser merges them into one.

```
<!DOCTYPE html>

<html>

  <head>

    <title>Learning HTML</title>

  </head>

  <body>

    <h1>Heading 1</h1> <!--This tag is used for heading size 1-->

    <p>

      Here is an example of how paragraphs<br> <!--<br> will be studied in upcoming chapters-->

      are added to an HTML page<br><!--the tag <br> is used to break line and move to the next line-->

    </p>

  </body>

</html>
```

Horizontal Lines:

The <hr> tag divides the page into parts, generating horizontal margins with the aid of a horizontal line that runs from the left to the right side of the page. There is indeed a null tag that accepts no further comments.

Text 1

_____

Text 2

```
<body>

    <h1>Heading 1</h1>

    <p>Text 1</p>

    <hr><!--This tag is used for horizontal line-->

    <p>Text 2</p>

  </body>
```


 Tag:

Using the <br> tag, you can tell HTML where the browser needs to change the points. There is no closing tag on these marks. As a result, changing the line with only one opening tag is possible.

HTML Images:

Any picture is inserted into the web page using the image attribute. The picture source is placed inside the image tag,

Inserting Images

and it is automatically displayed on the web page. The img src tag contains the basis of the picture.

Syntax: <img src="image-source">

```
<!DOCTYPE html>

<html>

  <head>

    <title>Learning HTML</title>

  </head>

  <body>

    <h2>Inserting Images</h2>

    <img src="https://sites.google.com/site/ictwoodlane/_/rsrc/
1299843628681/home/Google%20image.tiff">

  </body>

</html>
```

Lists:

A list is a collection of short pieces of information, such as people's names, usually written or printed with a single item on each line and organized to make finding a specific item simple. There are three ways to define lists of data in HTML. There must be at least one list in any index.

Following are the different types of lists in HTML:

ul	A list that is not in any order. It lists items by using bullets.	
ol	A list that is in numerical order. It will list the items using various numbering schemes.	
dl	A list of definitions. It puts the elements in an identical order as they will be in a dictionary.	

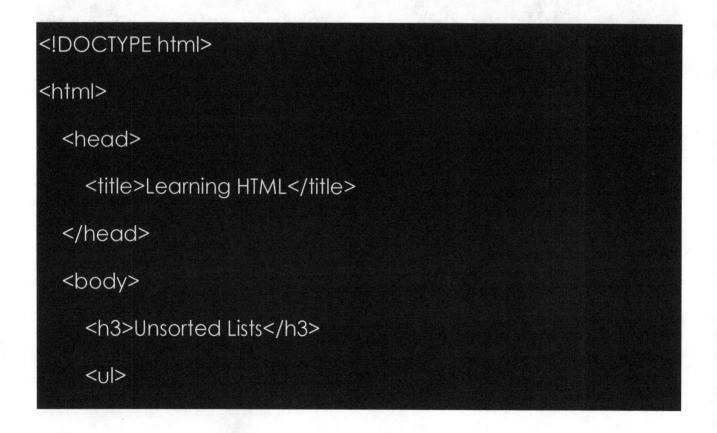

```html
<!DOCTYPE html>
<html>
  <head>
    <title>Learning HTML</title>
  </head>
  <body>
    <h3>Unsorted Lists</h3>
    <ul>
```

```html
    <li>HTML</li>

    <li>CSS</li>

    <li>JavaScripting</li>

  </ul>

  <h3>Sorted Lists</h3>

  <ol>

    <li>HTML</li>

    <li>CSS</li>

    <li>JavaScripting</li>

  </ol>

  <h3>Description Lists</h3>

  <dl>

    <dt>HTML</dt>

    <dd>- Hyper Text Markup Language</dd>

    <dt>CSS</dt>

    <dd>- Cascaded Style Sheets</dd>

  </dl>

  </body>

</html>
```

Here is how the output of the web page will look like:

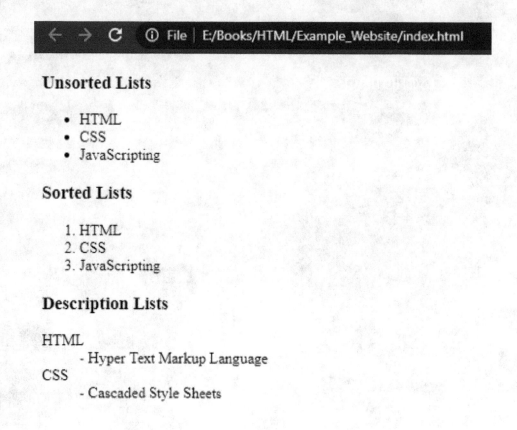

2.4: HTML Attributes

HTML attributes are special terms used inside the opening tag to control the entity's behavior. HTML attributes are a type of HTML feature modifier. An attribute either modifies an element type's default functionality or adds functionality to those element types that would otherwise be unable to function properly. An attribute is applied to an HTML start tag in HTML syntax.

It needs two inputs: a name and a value. These are located within the element's opening tag and describe the element's properties. The value parameter takes the property's value or the extent of the property titles that can be combined over the product, and the name parameter takes the name of the property we choose to assign to the element.

When used to change various entity types, certain attribute types behave differently. The attribute name, for example, is used by many element groups but serves slightly different purposes in each.

Syntax: <element attribute-name="attribute-value">

Following are some of the most widely used HTML attributes:

1. src Attribute:

The src attribute and the <img> tag are used to add an image into a webpage. Inside the double quotation, we must state the image's address as the attribute's value. Two easy to add links to a webpage are:

- **External URL:** This is a link to an external picture hosted onto an alternative website.

- **Relative URL:** This is a link to a picture hosted on the website. The domain name is not used in this URL. The URL would be in relation to the present page if it does not begin with a slash.

```
<!DOCTYPE html>

<html>

  <head>

    <title>Learning HTML</title>

  </head>

  <body>

    <h2>Inserting Images</h2>

    <img src="https://sites.google.com/site/ictwoodlane/_/rsrc/
1299843628681/home/Google%20image.tiff">

  </body>

</html>
```

2. alt Attribute:

This is an alternative tag that is used to show or display something if the primary attribute, namely the <img> tag, fails to display the value assigned to it. This can also be used to explain the picture to a creator on the other side of the screen.

```
<!DOCTYPE html>

<html>
```

```
<head>
    <title>Learning HTML</title>
</head>
<body>
    <h2>Inserting Images</h2>
    <img src="https://sites.goog/ictwoodlane/_/rsrc/1299843628
681/home/Google%20image.tiff" alt="Image Not Found">
</body>
</html>
```

The webpage will display:

Inserting Images

Image Not Found

3. Width and Height Attribute:

This parameter is used to adjust the image's width and height. It is used along with the <img> attribute.

```
<!DOCTYPE html>
<html>
    <head>
```

```
    <title>Learning HTML</title>

  </head>

  <body>

    <h2>Inserting Images</h2>

    <img src="image_1.jpg" width="420" height="240">

  </body>

</html>
```

The image displayed here is from a Relative URL, and its width and height can be set accordingly.

Inserting Images

4. The id Attribute:

This Attribute is utilized to give an entity a unique identifier. There will be times when we need to reach a particular feature with a familiar name. In that case, we assign different ids to different elements so that they can be viewed separately. The properties that expand the use of id are commonly found in CSS, which we will hear about later.

```html
<!DOCTYPE html>

<html>

  <head>

    <title>Learning HTML</title>

  </head>

  <body>

    <p id = "GfG">HTML Program<br>

    <p id = "ui">This is an example program.<br>

    <p id = "head">This is also a different example paragraph

  </body>

</html>
```

5. Title Attribute:

When the mouse is hovered over an aspect, the title attribute is used to describe it. The behavior varies depending on the element, but the value is usually displayed when loading or when the mouse pointer is hovered over it.

```html
<html>

  <head>

    <title>Learning HTML</title>

  </head>

  <body>

    <h3 title="Learn how to code">Hyper Text Markup Language</h3>

  </body>

</html>
```

Here is how the text will appear when the cursor hovers over it:

Hyper Text Markup Language

Learn how to code

6. The href Attribute:

This Attribute is used to define any address as a reference. This tag is used in conjunction with the <a> title. The text displayed inside the <a> tag is linked to the link placed in the href Attribute.

You will be routed to the page after clicking on the link. By default, the link opens in the same tag, but if we use the target attribute and set its value to "_blank," you will be redirected to a new tab or window, depending on the browser's settings.

```html
<!DOCTYPE html>
<html>
  <head>
    <title>Learning HTML</title>
  </head>
  <body>
    <a href="https://www.google.com/">
      Clicking on this text will open the website mentioned in the href attribute.
    </a><br>
    <a href="https://www.google.com/" target="_blank">
      Clicking on this text will open the website mentioned in a new tab.
    </a>
  </body>
</html>
```

The text will now appear as hyperlinked text, and by clicking on them, a new website will be opened.

Clicking on this text will open the website mentioned in the href attribute.
Clicking on this text will open the website mentioned in a new tab.

7. The style Attribute:

This attribute is used to apply CSS (Cascading Style Sheets) effects to HTML elements, such as the font size, modifying font family, and coloring, among other things. The following program displays a few names and values associated with the style attribute.

```html
<!DOCTYPE html>

<html>

  <head>

    <title>Learning HTML</title>

  </head>

  <body>

    <h3 style="font-size:30px;"> HTML.</h3>

    <h2 style="color:#8CCEF9;">CSS</h2>

    <h2 style="text-align:center">JAVA</h2>

  </body>
```

```
</html>
```

8. The lang Attribute:

The lang attribute specifies the vocabulary. Declaring a language is useful for search engines and accessibility applications. In the lang attribute, country codes may be added to the language code. As a result, the first two characters specify the HTML page's language, while the last two specify the region.

```
<!DOCTYPE html>
<html lang="en">
<head>
    <title>Learning HTML</title>
</head>
```

The HTML specification doesn't require lowercase attribute labels. Attributes may be written in capital letters or lowercase letters, such as title or TITLE. Though, it is recommended lower case letter attributes in HTML and requests lowercase attributes so it can be utilized for more substantial document kinds like XHTML.

The HTML specification doesn't entail quotes around attribute values. The W3C, on the other hand, recommends quotations in HTML and needs them in stricter text styles like XHTML.

2.5: Charsets

The alphabets, numbers, and certain other symbols are shown correctly by the web browser. All of this is possible thanks to the web browser's requisite character collection. The character set, also known as character encoding, has various character encoding specifications that assign numbers to the different characters found on the internet.

ASCII:

The American Standard Code provided this character encoding for Information Interchange (ANSII). In C/C++ programming, this character encoding is used. It contains 128 alphanumeric characters, including alphabets (A-Z) and (a-z) as well as special symbols such as + – * / ( ) @ and others.

ISO-8859:

HTML4 uses it as the default character set, and it supports 256 characters. The International Organization for Standardization (ISO) establishes character sets for various alphabets and languages. It includes numbers, upper and lowercase English letters, as well as certain special characters.

```
<meta http-equiv="Content_Type" content="text/html;charset=ISO-8859-1">
```

UFT-8:

Since the ISO-8859-character sets are narrow and incompatible in a multilingual setting, the Unicode Consortium created the UTF-8 and UTF-16 standards. It contains all of the punctuation and character marks.

```
<meta charset="UTF-8">
```

Chapter 3: Basic Rules and Practical Applications

3.1: Semantic Elements

Semantic HTML is a form of HTML that focuses on the meaning of the encoded data rather than its appearance (look). HTML has always included semantic markup, but it now includes presentational markup like the <font>, and < center> marks. The semantically neutral span and div tags are also available. Since the late 1990s, when most browsers began to support Cascading Style Sheets, web developers have been advised to stop using presentational HTML markup to keep presentation and content apart.

Semantic elements have descriptive names that indicate the content category. For instance, headers, footers, tables, and so on. HTML5 introduces dozens of new semantic features, as mentioned below that make code better to access and understand for developers while also instructing browsers on how to handle them.

1. Article:

It includes content that is self-contained and does not need any additional explanation. For example, a blog post, a newspaper article, and so on.

```html
<!DOCTYPE html>

<html lang="en">

<head>

  <title>Learning HTML</title>

  <style>

    body {

      text-align: center;

    }


    h1 {

      color: blueviolet;

    }

  </style>

</head>

<body>

  <article>

    <h1>Learning HTML</h1>

    <p>This is an example of articles.</p>

  </article>
```

```
</body>

</html>
```

2. Headers:

This is for the header of a page's introductory line, as the name implies. There can be several headers on a list.

```html
<!DOCTYPE html>

<html lang="en">

<head>

  <title>Learning HTML</title>

  <style>

    body {

      text-align: center;

    }


    h1 {

      color: blueviolet;

    }

  </style>

</head>
```

```
<body>

  <header>

    <h1>Learning HTML</h1>

    <p>This is an example of headers.</p>

  </header>

</body>

</html>
```

Here is how the webpage screen will look like:

Learning HTML

This is an example of headers.

3. Footers:

The footer is a section at the bottom of any article or document that may provide contact information, copyright information, and other information. On a page, there may be several footers.

```
<!DOCTYPE html>

<html lang="en">

<head>

  <title>Learning HTML</title>

  <style>
```

```
    body {

        text-align: center;

    }


    h1 {

        color: blueviolet;

    }

  </style>

</head>

<body>

  <footer>

    <p>Learning HTML</p>

    <p>This is an example of footers.</p>

  </footer>

</body>

</html>
```

4. Section:

A page may be divided into sections such as an introduction, contact information, and details, with each section having its own section name.

```html
!DOCTYPE html>
<html lang="en">
<head>
    <title>Learning HTML</title>
    <style>
        body {
            text-align: center;
        }

        h1 {
            color: blueviolet;
        }
    </style>
</head>
<body>
```

```
    <section>

       <h2>Learning HTML</h2>

       <p>This is an example of section.</p>

    </section>

    <section>

       <h2>Learning HTML</h2>

       <p>This is an example of section.</p>

    </section>

</body>

</html>
```

5. Nav:

It is used to create a navigation bar or nav menu that contains a series of connections.

```
<!DOCTYPE html>

<html lang="en">

<head>

</head>

<body>
```

```html
<h1>Navigation Bar for Main Page</h1>
  <nav>
    <a href="/home/">Home</a> |
    <a href="/about-us/">About Us</a> |
    <a href="/data-structure/">Contact</a> |
    <a href="/operating-system/">Review</a>
  </nav>
</body>
</html>
```

Non-Semantic Elements:

Tags like div and span are classified as non-semantic because their names don't indicate what kind of material is included. Each HTML element includes a default demonstration attribute that is determined by the element class. Most components include the default demonstration value of block or inline.

1. Block-level Elements:

Beginning on a separate line; block-level elements often extends as far as it can in each direction. The <div> element is the most used block-level element. It is used to hold other HTML elements in place. It does not have any prerequisites. The most widely used attributes are style, as well as class and id.

```html
<!DOCTYPE html>

<html lang="en">

<head>

  <title>Learning HTML</title>

</head>

<body>

  <style>

    body {

      text-align: center;

    }


    h1 {

      color: blueviolet;

    }

  </style>


  <!-- here the div element is used -->
```

```
    <div style="background-
color:black; color:white; padding:20px;">

        <h1>HTML</h1>

        <h3>CSS</h3>

        <h3>JAVA</h3>

    </div>

</body>

</html>
```

2. Inline Elements:

These elements do not begin on a separate line and just takes up the space needed. The most used inline element is <span>. The span element serves as a text container. It does not have any prerequisites. The most widely used attributes are style, as well as class and id.

```
<!DOCTYPE html>

<html lang="en">

<head>

  <title>Learning HTML</title>

</head>

<body>
```

```
<!-- here the span element is used -->

<h1>Learning<span style="color:#eeff00">HTML</span>today
</h1>

 </div>

</body>

</html>
```

Excellent lexical quality HTML also makes online documents more available. When screen readers or audio browser may accurately determine the layout of a text, it would not waste the visual impairment user's time by reading out redundant or meaningless material if the document has been appropriately marked up.

3.2: HTML Links

A link is referred to as a connection between two web resources. An anchor and a path are the two ends of a link. The link begins with the "source" anchor and leads to the "destination" anchor, which may be an image, a video clip, an audio file, a program, an HTML document, or an entity inside an HTML document.

Syntax: <a href="any URL"> Text over the link </a>

The href is used to identify the link's destination address. The visible portion of the connection is the text link. An internal link is a form of a hyperlink that points to a resource on the same website or domain, such as an image or text. Whereas an external link is any hyperlink from outside sources.

Multiple types of links can be found in a variety of formats, including:

- By default, an unvisited path is underlined and blue.

- By default, a visited path is underlined and purple.

- By default, an active path is underlined and red.

CSS may be used to adjust the appearance of connections.

Syntax: <img src="URL" alt="some-text">

- **src**: Source is abbreviated as src. The src attribute on any image tells the browser where to look for the image you want to view. The given URL for the image leads to the image's storage site.

- **alt**: If the icon cannot be seen, the alt attribute serves as an alternate definition. The alt attribute's meaning is a user-defined document.

Images:

Setting parameters of an image: The height and weight of an image are defined using the width and height attributes. By default, attribute values are listed in pixels, as mentioned in the previous chapter.

Adding animated images: The "img" tag can also be used to add animated icons in the .gif format.

```
<img src = "HTML.gif" alt = "HTML" style = "width:200px; height:200px;">
```

Adding titles to Image: Titles may be attached to images in addition to the pictures themselves to provide more detail about the embedded file. The title attribute is used to insert a title.

```
<img src = "HTML.jpg" alt = "HTML" style = "width:200px; height:200px;" title="Learning HTML">
```

Adding images as links: Any picture with a URL embedded in it can be used as a guide. It is possible to do so by putting a <img> tag inside an <a> tag.

```
<a href="https://www.google.com/">
<img src = "HTML.jpg" alt = "HTML" style = "width:200px; height:200px;" title="Learning HTML">
</a>
```

By clicking on the image, the user will be redirected to the website stated in the href Attribute.

Using background images: A website may have a picture as a backdrop as well.

```html
<body style="background-image:url
('https://www.finsmes.com/wp-
content/uploads/2016/09/google.jpg')">


    <h2>Image as Background</h2>


    <p>In this example an image is placed as background.</p>
</body>
```

Using Iframes:

In HTML, iframe stands for Inline Frame. The <iframe> tag designates a rectangular area inside a document where the browser will view a different composition, complete with scroll bars and borders. An inline frame is a type of HTML document that allows you to add another form within it. The 'src 'attribute specifies the URL of the text that will be displayed in the iframe. It is also used to embed data onto the web page in videos, images, or maps.

The iframe's size is determined by the height and width attributes. By default, attribute values are specified in pixels, but they can also be set in percentages, such as "80%".

```
<iframe height="720" width="1280"src="https://www.youtube.com/embed/XZ1NcwErw2s">
```

Iframes have a boundary around them by default. We must use the style attribute and the CSS border property to delete the border.

```
<iframe height="720" width="1280"src="https://www.youtube.com/embed/XZ1NcwErw2s" style="border:none">
```

3.3: HTML Forms

HTML Form is a document that uses interactive controls to store user information on a web server. An HTML form may contain various data, such as a username, password, phone number, and email address. Checkboxes, input boxes, radio keys, send buttons, and other features are used in HTML forms. The knowledge of a customer is sent to a web server using these components. To make an HTML form, we use the form tag.

Basic forms are coded someway like this:

```
<!DOCTYPE html>
```

```html
<html>

<body>

<form>

 Name:<br>

 <input type="text" name="user-name">

 <br>

 Email:<br>

 <input type="text" name="email">

 <br><br>

 <input type="submit" value="Submit">

</form>

</body>

</html>
```

Input Element in forms:

The essential elements used in HTML Forms are input elements. Text fields, checkboxes, password fields, radio buttons, submit buttons, and other user input fields can be generated. The following are the most common input elements:

1. Text Field:

The text field is a single-line input field where the user will type text. The "data" variable is used to construct Text Field input controls, with the form attribute set to "text."

```html
<!DOCTYPE html>

<html>

<h3>This is an example of text field forms</h3>

<body>

  <form>

    <label for="EMAIL">Email:</label><br>

    <input type="text" name="Email" id="Email">

  </form>

</body>

</html>
```

Here is how the webpage output looks like:

This is an example of text field forms

Email: [   ]

2. Password Field:

Password fields are a kind of text field in which the data entered is obscured with asterisks or dots to prevent any person from seeing the user's identification. The "input" variable is used to construct password field input controls, with the form attribute set to "password."

```
<!DOCTYPE html>

<html>

<h3>This is an example of Password Field in HTML Forms</h3>

<body>

  <form>

    <label for="user-password">User Password:

    </label><br>

    <input type="password" name="user-
pass" id="user_password">

  </form>

</body>

</html>
```

Here is how the webpage output looks like:

This is an example of Password Field in HTML Forms

User Password:

3. Radio Buttons:

The user will choose precisely one choice from a list of predefined choices using radio buttons. The "data" variable with the type attribute set to "radio" is used to construct radio button input controls.

```
<!DOCTYPE html>

<html>

<h3>This is an example of Radio Buttons in forms</h3>

<body>

  <form>

    SELECT LANGUAGE

    <br>

    <input type="radio" name="language" id="HTML">

    <label for="HTML">HTML</label><br>

    <input type="radio" name="language" id="CSS">

    <label for="CSS">CSS</label>
```

```
    </form>

</body>

</html>
```

Here is how the webpage output looks like:

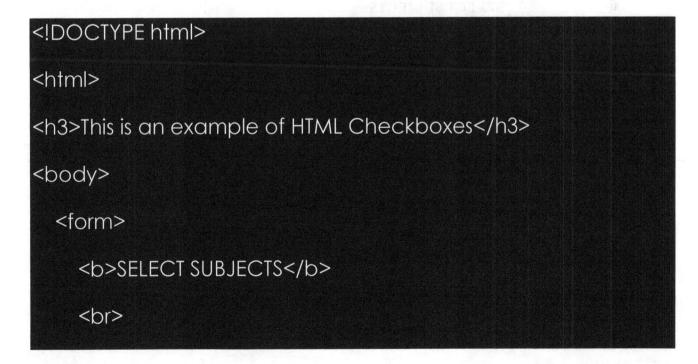

4. Checkboxes:

Checkboxes enable the user to choose one or more choices from a list of pre-defined options. The "data" variable with the form attribute set to "checkbox" is used to construct checkbox input controls.

```
<!DOCTYPE html>

<html>

<h3>This is an example of HTML Checkboxes</h3>

<body>

  <form>

    <b>SELECT SUBJECTS</b>

    <br>
```

```html
    <input type="checkbox" name="subject" id="computers">

    <label for="computers">Computers</label>

    <input type="checkbox" name="subject" id="latin">

    <label for="latin">Latin</label>

    <input type="checkbox" name="subject" id="english">

    <label for="english">English</label>

  </form>

</body>

</html>
```

Here is how the webpage output looks like:

This is an example of HTML Checkboxes

SELECT SUBJECTS
☐ Computers ☐ Latin ☑ English

5. File Select Boxes:

File select boxes enable users to select a local file and send it to the webserver as an attachment. It looks like a text box with a button that lets the user search for a file. The location and name of the file can also be written instead of browsing for it. The "input" variable is used to generate select file boxes, with the form attribute set to "file."

```
<!DOCTYPE html>

<html>

<h3>This is an example of a File Select Box</3>

  <body>

  <form>

    <label for="fileselect">Upload:</label>

    <input type="file" name="upload" id="fileselect">

  </form>

</body>

</html>
```

Here is how the webpage output looks like:

This is an example of a File Select Box
Upload: [Choose File] No file chosen

6. Text-area:

It is a multi-line text input control that enables the user to enter a definition or text through several lines. The "textarea" element is used to construct a Text Area input control.

```
<!DOCTYPE html>

<html>
```

```
<h3>This is an example of a Text Area Box</h3>

<body>

  <form>

    <label for="Text">Text:</label>

    <textarea rows="4" cols="40" name="Text" id="Text"></textarea>

  </form>

</body>

</html>
```

Here is how the webpage output looks like:

This is an example of a Text Area Box

Text:

7. Select Boxes:

Select boxes are often used to enable consumers to choose one or more alternatives from a drop-down menu of choices. Pick boxes are made up of two components: "select" and "choice." The select factor defines the list elements.

```
<!DOCTYPE html>
```

```html
<html>

<h3>This is an example of a Select Box</h3>

<body>

  <form>

    <label for="country">Country:</label>

    <select name="country" id="country">

      <option value="Canada">Canada</option>

      <option value="Australia">Australia</option>

      <option value="China">China</option>

    </select>

  </form>

</body>

</html>
```

Here is how the webpage output looks like:

This is an example of a Select Box

8. Submit and Reset Buttons:

The Submit Button allows the user to transfer the information from the form to the web server. The Reset Button is used to clear the form data and return it to its default state.

```
<!DOCTYPE html>

<html>

<h3>This is an example of a submit and reset buttons</h3>

<body>

    <form action="test.php" method="post" id="users">

        <label for="user-name">User-name:</label>

        <input type="text" name="user-name" id="User-name">

        <input type="submit" value="Submit">

        <input type="reset" value="Reset">

    </form>

</body>

</html>
```

Here is how the webpage output looks like:

This is an example of a submit and reset buttons

User-name: [＿＿＿＿＿＿＿＿＿] [Submit] [Reset]

3.4: CSS along with HTML

Cascading Style Sheets is a web development scripting language used to form HTML elements viewed as a web page in browsers. The website built with HTML will appear dull if CSS is not used. CSS, in a nutshell, gives every HTML feature a protective shell. If you think of HTML as the skeleton of a web page, CSS is the skin that covers it. Text/CSS is the Internet media sort (MIME type) for CSS. The CSS standard was created by the World Wide Web Consortium (W3C) in 1996. CSS can be used to style HTML documents in a variety of ways.

CSS is a style sheet that allows you to separate presentation from text which includes layout, colors, and fonts. By separating them it will provide necessities approachability, more control and flexibility in the condition of performance characteristics and allow several web pages to exchange formatting by defining the applicable CSS in a separate file that is named with the extension .css, which handles recurrence in the basic content and allows the .css file to improve page loading speed.

CSS is used along with HTML for the many following reasons:

- **Time-Saving:** CSS saves time because it allows you to write CSS once and reuse it through several HTML pages.

- **Simple to maintain:** To make a global adjustment, change the theme, and all items on all web pages will be immediately changed.

- **Search Engines:** CSS is a clean coding technique, which implies search engines can have a much easier time "reading" the text.

- **Superior styles over HTML:** CSS has a far more extensive set of attributes than HTML because then you can give the HTML page a much better look than HTML attributes.

- **Offline Browsing:** With the aid of offline cache, CSS can hold web applications locally. We may use this to view websites that are not available online.

- **Selectors:** There are several selectors in CSS (ID selectors, Class Selectors, and so on) that can be used to execute various tasks.

CSS Syntax:

A CSS file is made up of style rules that the browser interprets and then applies to the elements in your text. A selector and declaration block make up a style rule package.

The following is an example of an inline CSS style:

```html
<h1 style="color: blue;">Learning HTML</h1>
```

The following is an example of how inline CSS will look in a program:

```html
<!DOCTYPE html>

<html>

 <head>

  <title> This is an example of internal CSS </title>

  <style>

  h1 {

    color:blue;

  }

  </style>

 <head>

 <body>

  <h1">Learning HTML</h1>

 </body>

</html>
```

Advantages of using CSS with HTML:

- CSS is cross-platform and device-agnostic.

- Website maintenance is fast and straightforward, thanks to CSS.

- CSS allows for both planned and unplanned modifications.

- CSS speeds up the website and improves the ability of search engines to index the pages.

- It has a unique attribute in that it can be repositioned.

Disadvantages of CSS:

- There is a cross-browser problem in CSS. If you build something and test it in Chrome, it might look great, but that does not mean it'll look the same in other browsers. Then you would also have the script for that browser.

- In CSS, there is a security flaw.

- CSS is insecure, which means it may be targeted.

- CSS has a problem with fragmentation.

CSS is divided into three categories, as seen below:

1. **Inline CSS**: Inline CSS adds style to tags by using the "style" attribute inside the tag we choose to design.

2. **CSS Embedded or Internal:** By putting the style> tag within the <head> tag, we can style our page with internal CSS. We apply the template that we want to our carrier within the <style> tag.

3. **External CSS:** We can use external CSS to add flair to our HTML page. We can put our styles in a separate file with the extension.css and connect it to our HTML tab.

CSS data can be obtained from a variety of sources. It can either be a web browser, a recipient, or an author. CSS style details can be contained in a different file or inserted inside an HTML document. Importing several style sheets is possible. Different formats can be used dependent on the display device; for instance, computer edition and the written edition could be very different, allowing writers to adapt the presentation to each format.

This book will only study inline CSS as it is a part of HTML and can be used correlatively. At the same time, CSS can also be imported from an external file by adding the file to the website folder and placing a statement at the start of the page regarding that CSS style sheet.

3.5: Responsive Web Design

The browser's view is the portion of a web page where the user can see the text. The viewport is not uniform in scale; it varies according to the computers' screen size on which the website is shown. In comparison to a smartphone or tablet, the viewport on a laptop is bigger.

On smaller screens, a website that is not sensitive for smaller viewports looks poor or even splits. Introduce a sensitive tag to monitor the viewport to solve this issue. Apple Inc. was the first to add this tag for Safari iOS.

Syntax: <meta name="viewport" content= "width=device-width, initial-scale=1.0">

It is the most popular viewport environment seen on mobile-friendly websites. The width property regulates the viewport's width. You can set them to a specific value ("width=600"). It is set to a special discount ("width= device-width"), the device's width in CSS pixels at a range of 100 percent. When a page is loaded as a test try, the initial-scale property determines the zoom degree. The meta tag is included in the HTML document's head tag.

The following is credited to a Responsive tag:

- **width**: The device's virtual viewport's width.

- **height**: The device's virtual viewport's height.

- **initial scale:** The zoom size when you first view the website.

- **minimum scale:** The smallest zoom size that a user can achieve on a website.

- **maximum scale:** The highest zoom level a user can achieve on a website.

- **user-scalable:** A flag that helps the user to zoom in or out on the screen.

```html
<!DOCTYPE html>

<html>

  <head>

    <title>Learning HTML</title>

    <meta charset="utf-8" name="viewport"

    content= "width=device-width, initial-scale=1.0">

    <style>

      .gfg {

        font-size:40px;

        font-weight:bold;
```

```
        color:blue;

        text-align:center;

    }

    .geeks {

        font-size:16px;

        text-align:center;

    }

    p {

        text-align:justify;

    }

    </style>

</head>

<body>

    <div class = "gfg">Learning HTML</div>

    <div class = "geeks">What is HTML?</div>

    <p>HyperText Markup Language, is the basic markup langu
age for documents that are intended to be used in a web brow
ser. Technology solutions like Cascading Style Sheets (CSS) and s
preadsheet programs like JavaScript may help.  Online used tha
```

```
t HTML documents from either a web server or locally stored files
 and convert them to interactive web pages. HTML originally pro
vided clues for the document's presentation and defined the la
yout of a web page semantically.</p>

        <p>HTML allows scripting languages like JavaScript to emb
ed programmes that affect the actions and content of web pa
ges. CSS determines the appearance and structure of text. Sinc
e 1997, the World Wide Web Consortium (W3C), which used to u
phold the HTML standards and now maintains the CSS standards
, has promoted the use of CSS over explicit presentational HTML.
 </p>

    </body>

</html>
```

Here is how the output screen will look with the meta tag

Learning HTML
What is HTML?

HTML, or HyperText Markup Language, is the basic markup language for documents that are intended to be used in a web browser. Technology solutions like Cascading Style Sheets (CSS) and spreadsheet programs like JavaScript may help. Online used that HTML documents from either a web server or locally stored files and convert them to interactive web pages. HTML originally provided clues for the document's presentation and defined the layout of a web page semantically.

HTML allows scripting languages like JavaScript to embed programmes that affect the actions and content of web pages. CSS determines the appearance and structure of text. Since 1997, the World Wide Web Consortium (W3C), which used to uphold the HTML standards and now maintains the CSS standards, has promoted the use of CSS over explicit presentational HTML.

The device width is set to wide display, and hence it will display a responsive output depending upon the device being used.

Images that scale well to suit any browser size are known as responsive pictures. A picture will scale up and down as the browser window is resized when the CSS width value is set to standard values.

```
<img src="imgage.jpg" style="width:80%;height:auto;">
```

The picture will scale down if necessary if the max-width property is set to 100 percent, but it will never scale up to be larger than its original height.

Chapter 4: Make your own HTML program

In this chapter, an example webpage will be explained using all the concepts presented in the above chapters. It provides you with an idea of how HTML programming works and broadens your view of how various tags and elements can form different styles and layouts.

A standard text editor will suffice for making websites. However, some editors make programming even more effortless. As a measure, a modern code editor is recommended.

Once the editor is all set up now an HTML file can be created:

- Make a folder for your project on your computer. It can be named anything accordingly.

- Now open Visual Studio Code.

- Pick Open Folder from the File menu and open the folder you created by searching for it.

- Click New File from the context menu by right-clicking below the folder. The file should be called index.html.

- You now have an HTML file.

As you might expect, the word index.html has a special meaning. The index.html file is immediately shown when a website address is named, and that file is also known as the main page or home page of a website.

It is a tourism promotion webpage that contains all the different aspects of a webpage and is complete. This code can be tried out on any computer; the only limitation is that some of the images would not be visible as they are device-linked images. The web page given in this chapter is explained using comments in detail.

Example Web page:

```
<!DOCTYPE html><!--
here the document is declared before the HTML code-->
<html lang="en"><!--
the language has been defined using lang attribute-->
<head><!--header files start from here-->
 <meta charset="UTF-8">
 <meta name="viewport" content="width=device-width, initial-scale=1.0"><!--
charset and viewport enables the interactive website for desktop-->
```

```html
<link href="https://unpkg.com/tailwindcss@^2/dist/tailwind.min.css" rel="stylesheet"><!--
external stylesheet can also be linked in head-->

  <title>My Trip Companion Pakistan</title><!--title of the page-->

  <header class="text-gray-700 body-font">

    <div class="container mx-auto flex p-5 flex-col flex-wrap md:flex-row items-center"><!--
these lines specify the indentation of the page or section being displayed-->

      <a class="flex title-font items-center font-medium text-gray-900 mb-4 md:mb-0">

        <img width="100px" height="100px" src="images\logo.jpg">
<!--an image from the device is used as the logo-->

        <span class="ml-3 text-xl text-500 tracking-widest">Trip Companion</span>

      </a>

      <nav class="md:mr-auto md:ml-4 md:py-1 md:pl-4 md:border-l md:border-gray-400 flex flex-wrap items-center text-base justify-center"><!--
here the header of a page is created using nav-->
```

```html
    <svg class="w-6 h-6" fill="none" stroke="currentColor" viewBox="0 0 24 24" xmlns="http://www.w3.org/2000/svg"><path stroke-linecap="round" stroke-linejoin="round" stroke-width="2" d="M3 12l2-2m0 0l7-7 7 7M5 10v10a1 1 0 001 1h3m10-11l2 2m-2-2v10a1 1 0 01-1 1h-3m-6 0a1 1 0 001-1v-4a1 1 0 011-1h2a1 1 0 011 1v4a1 1 0 001 1m-6 0h6"></path></svg><!--
an external link for an entity is used here-->

    <a class="mr-5 inline-flex items-center bg-white-200 border-0 py-1 px-3 focus:outline-none hover:bg-green-400 rounded text-base mt-4 md:mt-0" href="main.html">Home</a>

    <div class="dropdown"><!--
a dropdown menu is created using simple <a> tags-->

    <a class="mr-5 inline-flex items-center bg-white-100 border-0 py-1 px-3 focus:outline-none hover:bg-green-400 rounded text-base mt-4 md:mt-0"><!--styling the menu-->

    <button class="dropbtn" >Explore Pakistan</button></a><!--
a button is created which is clicked to open the dropdow menu
-->
```

```html
        <div class="dropdown-content">

        <a href="Punjab.html" class="px-2 py-1 hover:bg-green-300 rounded">Punjab</a>

        <a href="Sindh.html" class="px-2 py-1 hover:bg-green-300 rounded">Sindh</a>

        <a href="Khyber Pakhtunkhwa.html" class="px-2 py-1 hover:bg-green-300 rounded">Khyber-Pakhtunkhwa</a>

        <a href="Balochistan.html" class="px-2 py-1 hover:bg-green-300 rounded">Balochistan</a>

        <a href="Gilgit - Baltistan.html" class="px-2 py-1 hover:bg-green-300 rounded">Gilgit-Baltistan</a>

        <a href="Kashmir.html" class="px-2 py-1 hover:bg-green-300 rounded">Kashmir</a>

    </div>

    </div><!--
other header links are also displayed in the next lines-->

        <a class="mr-5 inline-flex items-center bg-white-200 border-0 py-1 px-3 focus:outline-none hover:bg-green-400 rounded text-base mt-4 md:mt-0" href="BLOG.HTML"> Blogs</a>
```

```html
    <a class="mr-5 inline-flex items-center bg-white-200 border-0 py-1 px-3 focus:outline-none hover:bg-green-400 rounded text-base mt-4 md:mt-0" href="takeyourtrip.html">Trips</a>

      <a class="mr-5 inline-flex items-center bg-white-200 border-0 py-1 px-3 focus:outline-none hover:bg-green-400 rounded text-base mt-4 md:mt-0" href="aboutus.html">About Us</a>

   </nav>

   <button class="inline-flex items-center bg-gray-200 border-0 py-1 px-3 focus:outline-none hover:bg-gray-300 rounded text-base mt-4 md:mt-0">

      <a href="takeyourtrip.html">Plan Your Trip</a>

      <svg fill="none" stroke-linecap="round" stroke-linejoin="round" stroke-width="2" class="w-4 h-4 ml-1" stroke="currentColor" viewBox="0 0 24 24">

        <path d="M5 12h14M12 5l7 7-7 7"></path>

      </svg>

   </button><!--
a button is created here to be directed to a different page on t
```

he same website, it will be unavailable to other computers as th
e file does not exist there-->

   </div>

   </header><!--
header nav ends here and anything after this is part of the simpl
e page-->

  <style><!--
internal style is used here to define the styles of the whole page-
->

   .dropbtn {

     color: rgb(10, 10, 10);

     padding: 2px;

     font-size: 16px;

     border: none;

     border-radius: 6px;

   }<!--this is for the dropdown menu in headers-->

   .dropdown {

     position: relative;

     display: inline-block;

```css
}

.dropdown-content {

  display: none;

  position: absolute;

  background-color: #f1f1f1;

  min-width: 80px;

  box-shadow: 0px 8px 16px 0px rgba(0,0,0,0.2);

  border-radius: 6px;

  z-index: 1;
}<!--to set the dropdown display-->


.dropdown-content a {

  color: black;

  padding: 8px 14px;

  text-decoration: none;

  display: block;
}<!--color of content in dropbox-->
```

```html
.dropdown-content a:hover {background-color: #ddd;}


.dropdown:hover .dropdown-content {display: block;}

</style>

<section class="text-gray-700 body-font">

  <div class="container px-5 py-24 mx-auto">

    <div class="flex flex-col text-center w-full mb-20"><!--
here the text title is displayed, its layout is set using multiple css st
atements and height width values-->

      <h1 class="sm:text-3xl text-2xl font-medium title-font mb-
2 text-gray-900 tracking-widest mb-
1">Trip Companion - where great journeys begin!</h1>

      <p class="lg:w-2/3 mx-auto leading-relaxed text-
base">Wondering how to plan next best trip? Don't Worry, we've
 got you covered.</p><!--
text in the form of paragragh is shown here-->

    </div><!--
div is used to add division between different sections of the cod
e, and it effects the layout-->
```

```html
<body><!--
the body tag indicates the start of the webpage body-->
 <section class="text-gray-700 body-font">

   <div class="container px-5 py-24 mx-auto"><!--
class is used to set the parameters of the text or data to be displ
ayed-->

     <div class="flex flex-col text-center w-full mb-20">

       <h1 class="sm:text-3xl text-2xl font-medium title-font font-
family sans-serif mb-2 text-gray-900 tracking-widest mb-
1"> EXPLORE PAKISTAN - With Trip Companion</h1><br><br><!--
heading is added using h1-->

       <p class="lg:w-2/3 mx-auto leading-relaxed text-
base"> Situated on the crossroads of South Asia, the Middle East
, and Central Asia, <br>Pakistan is a beautiful country with a uni
que history and cultural heritage.<br> Pakistan was the site for o
ne of the world's earliest human settlements:<br> the great prehi
storic Indus Valley Civilization, the crucible of ancient empires, re
ligions <br>and cultures. The land of Pakistan ranges from lofty
mountains in the north,<br> the Karakorum and the Himalayas, t
hrough dissected plateaus to the rich alluvial<br> plains of the P
unjab. Then follows the desolate barrenness of Baluchistan and t
```

he hot, dry
deserts of Sindh blending into miles and miles of golden beaches of Makran coast. </p>

<hr>

</div><!--a paragraph is displayed here-->

<section class="text-gray-700 body-font">

<div class="container px-5 py-24 mx-auto">

<div class="flex flex-col text-center w-full mb-20">

<h1 class="sm:text-3xl text-2xl font-medium title-font mb-2 text-gray-900 tracking-widest mb-1"> B L O G S</h1>

<p class="lg:w-2/3 mx-auto leading-relaxed text-base">Inspiration for your next trip! </p>

<section class="text-gray-700 body-font"><!--this section is layed out such that it displays 3 boxes in the form of blogs-->

<div class="container px-5 py-24 mx-auto">

<div class="flex flex-wrap -m-4">

<div class="p-4 md:w-1/3">

<div class="h-full border-2 border-gray-200 rounded-lg overflow-hidden"><!--sets the borders of te first blog box-->

<img class="lg:h-48 md:h-36 w-full object-cover object-center" src="https://i.pinimg.com/564x/d4/d9/05/d4d905f5cb0a

10241791a1413b35ef72.jpg " alt="blog"><!--
an image is linked here for a blog post-->

        <div class="p-6">

        <h2 class="tracking-widest text-xs title-font font-
medium text-gray-500 mb-1">Blog Post</h2>

        <h1 class="title-font text-lg font-medium text-gray-
900 mb-3"><u> 10 Must Visit Places in Islamabad</u></h1><!--
the <u> tag underlines the text inside it-->

        <p class="leading-relaxed mb-
3"> Islamabad is a beautiful, clean and lush green capital of Pak
istan. It is no wonder it is considered the 2nd most beautiful capi
tal in the world. </p>

<!--adds spaces inbetween lines-->

        <div class="flex items-center flex-wrap ">

        <a class="text-green-500 inline-flex items-
center md:mb-2 lg:mb-0" href="https://www.doseoflife.com/10-
must-visit-places-in-islamabad/">Read More<!--
here a link is added under Read More, when it is clicked the link
ed page will open-->

        <svg class="w-4 h-4 ml-
2" viewBox="0 0 24 24" stroke="currentColor" stroke-

```
width="2" fill="none" stroke-linecap="round" stroke-
linejoin="round">

        <path d="M5 12h14"></path>

        <path d="M12 5l7 7-7 7"></path>

    </svg>

    </a>

    <span class="text-gray-600 mr-3 inline-flex items-
center lg:ml-auto md:ml-0 ml-auto leading-none text-sm pr-3 py-
1 border-r-2 border-gray-300">

        <svg class="w-4 h-4 mr-1" stroke="currentColor" stroke-
width="2" fill="none" stroke-linecap="round" stroke-
linejoin="round" viewBox="0 0 24 24">

        <path d="M1 12s4-8 11-8 11 8 11 8-4 8-11 8-11-8-11-
8z"></path>

        <circle cx="12" cy="12" r="3"></circle>

    </svg>1.2K

    </span><!--
these are the small entities at the bottom of the blog box-->

    <span class="text-gray-600 inline-flex items-
center leading-none text-sm">
```

```
        <svg class="w-4 h-4 mr-1" stroke="currentColor" stroke-
width="2" fill="none" stroke-linecap="round" stroke-
linejoin="round" viewBox="0 0 24 24">
        <path d="M21 11.5a8.38 8.38 0 01-.9 3.8 8.5 8.5 0 01-
7.6 4.7 8.38 8.38 0 01-3.8-.9L3 21l1.9-5.7a8.38 8.38 0 01-.9-
3.8 8.5 8.5 0 014.7-7.6 8.38 8.38 0 013.8-
.9h.5a8.48 8.48 0 018 8v.5z"></path>
        </svg>6
    </span><!--span is used for the entities-->
    </div>
    </div>
    </div>
    </div>
    <div class="p-4 md:w--1/3"><!--
here again just like above another blog box is created-->
        <div class="h-full border-2 border-gray-200 rounded-
lg overflow-hidden">
        <img class="lg:h-48 md:h-36 w-full object-cover object-
center" src="https://i.pinimg.com/564x/5b/e0/a1/5be0a1ed96a
08ca894ded774cc4f5acb.jpg" alt="blog"><!--image link-->
```

```html
<div class="p-6">

    <h2 class="tracking-widest text-xs title-font font-medium text-gray-500 mb-1">Blog Post</h2><!--heading-->

    <h1 class="title-font text-lg font-medium text-gray-900 mb-3"><u>Pakistan through the eyes of travelers</u></h1>

    <p class="leading-relaxed mb-3">It was another visa run visit to Pakistan. My second one this year so far. It was a short trip, long enough to be bored at home doing nothing but too short to explore Pakistan like I did in the previous visit.</p>

    <br><br>

    <div class="flex items-center flex-wrap">

    <a class="text-green-500 inline-flex items-center md:mb-2 lg:mb-0" href="https://www.doseoflife.com/explore-pakistan-travel-bloggers/">Read More<!--link for the blog is added here-->

    <svg class="w-4 h-4 ml-2" viewBox="0 0 24 24" stroke="currentColor" stroke-width="2" fill="none" stroke-linecap="round" stroke-linejoin="round">

    <path d="M5 12h14"></path>
```

```html
    <path d="M12 5l7 7-7 7"></path>

   </svg>

  </a><!--entities are used to created small icons-->

  <span class="text-gray-600 mr-3 inline-flex items-center lg:ml-auto md:ml-0 ml-auto leading-none text-sm pr-3 py-1 border-r-2 border-gray-300">

   <svg class="w-4 h-4 mr-1" stroke="currentColor" stroke-width="2" fill="none" stroke-linecap="round" stroke-linejoin="round" viewBox="0 0 24 24">

    <path d="M1 12s4-8 11-8 11 8 11 8-4 8-11 8-11-8-11-8z"></path>

    <circle cx="12" cy="12" r="3"></circle>

   </svg>1.2K

  </span>

  <span class="text-gray-600 inline-flex items-center leading-none text-sm">

   <svg class="w-4 h-4 mr-1" stroke="currentColor" stroke-width="2" fill="none" stroke-linecap="round" stroke-linejoin="round" viewBox="0 0 24 24">
```

```
            <path d="M21 11.5a8.38 8.38 0 01-.9 3.8 8.5 8.5 0 01-
7.6 4.7 8.38 8.38 0 01-3.8-.9L3 21l1.9-5.7a8.38 8.38 0 01-.9-
3.8 8.5 8.5 0 014.7-7.6 8.38 8.38 0 013.8-
.9h.5a8.48 8.48 0 018 8v.5z"></path>

          </svg>6

          </span>

        </div>

      </div>

      </div>

   </div><!--second blog box ends here-->

   <div class="p-4 md:w-1/3">

     <div class="h-full border-2 border-gray-200 rounded-
lg overflow-hidden">

       <img class="lg:h-48 md:h-36 w-full object-cover object-
center" src="https://i.pinimg.com/564x/fd/72/c8/fd72c85fd3d3a
7ccef8a6c3c3e8c569b.jpg" alt="blog">

       <br><div class="p-6">

         <h2 class="tracking-widest text-xs title-font font-
medium text-gray-500 mb-1">Blog Posts</h2>
```

```html
<h1 class="title-font text-lg font-medium text-gray-900 mb-3"><u>Planning your trip to Snow in Pakistan</u> </h1>

        <p class="leading-relaxed mb-3">If you are planning a trip to the snowy mountains, Choosing the best travel guide would be your first priority. The popular resorts of Malam Jabba and Naltar Valley offer skiing and snowboarding for all abilities</p><br>

        <div class="flex items-center flex-wrap "><!--this wraps the image or entities in that specific area-->

        <a class="text-green-500 inline-flex items-center md:mb-2 lg:mb-0" href="https://www.pakistantravelguide.pk/2020/12/16/planning-your-trip-to-snow-in-pakistan/">Read More

        <svg class="w-4 h-4 ml-2" viewBox="0 0 24 24" stroke="currentColor" stroke-width="2" fill="none" stroke-linecap="round" stroke-linejoin="round">

        <path d="M5 12h14"></path>

        <path d="M12 5l7 7-7 7"></path>

    </svg>

    </a>
```

```html
<span class="text-gray-600 mr-3 inline-flex items-center lg:ml-auto md:ml-0 ml-auto leading-none text-sm pr-3 py-1 border-r-2 border-gray-300">
  <svg class="w-4 h-4 mr-1" stroke="currentColor" stroke-width="2" fill="none" stroke-linecap="round" stroke-linejoin="round" viewBox="0 0 24 24">
    <path d="M1 12s4-8 11-8 11 8 11 8-4 8-11 8-11-8-11-8z"></path>
    <circle cx="12" cy="12" r="3"></circle>
  </svg>1.2K
</span>
<span class="text-gray-600 inline-flex items-center leading-none text-sm">
  <svg class="w-4 h-4 mr-1" stroke="currentColor" stroke-width="2" fill="none" stroke-linecap="round" stroke-linejoin="round" viewBox="0 0 24 24">
    <path d="M21 11.5a8.38 8.38 0 01-.9 3.8 8.5 8.5 0 01-7.6 4.7 8.38 8.38 0 01-3.8-.9L3 21l1.9-5.7a8.38 8.38 0 01-.9-3.8 8.5 8.5 0 014.7-7.6 8.38 8.38 0 013.8-.9h.5a8.48 8.48 0 018 8v.5z"></path>
  </svg>6
```

```html
        </span>

      </div>

    </div>

   </div>

  </div>

 </div><hr><!--

horizontal rule adds a line at the end of the section-->

 <section class="text-gray-700 body-font"><!--

this section different images are displayed in the form of a galler
y-->

   <div class="container px-5 py-24 mx-auto flex flex-wrap">

   <div class="flex w-full mb-20 flex-wrap">

    <h1 class="sm:text-3xl text-2xl font-medium title-font text-
gray-900 lg:w-1/3 lg:mb-0 mb-4"> S C E N I C - B E A U T Y </h1>

     <p class="lg:pl-6 lg:w-2/3 mx-auto leading-relaxed text-
base"></p>

   </div>

   <div class="flex flex-wrap md:-m-2 -m-1">

   <div class="flex flex-wrap w--1/2">
```

```html
<div class="md:p-2 p-1 w-1/2"><!--
images are placed inside class tags-->

    <img alt="gallery" class="w-full object-cover h-full object-center block" src="https://i.pinimg.com/564x/29/08/32/290832d040b988e492aebaacecba66b9.jpg">

  </div>

  <div class="md:p-2 p-1 w-1/2">

    <img alt="gallery" class="w-full object-cover h-full object-center block" src="https://i.pinimg.com/564x/d0/ec/01/d0ec012743b2ca35850acb7d845eec49.jpg">

  </div>

  <div class="md:p-2 p-1 w-full">

    <img alt="gallery" class="w-full h-full object-cover object-center block" src="https://www.beltroad-initiative.com/wp-content/uploads/2018/06/ronan-680083-unsplash_klein-825x510.jpg">

  </div>

</div><!--it sets the order of images-->

<div class="flex flex-wrap w-1/2">

  <div class="md:p-2 p-1 w-full">
```

```html
    <img alt="gallery" class="w-full h-full object-cover object-center block" src="https://www.nationalgeographic.com/content/dam/news/2015/12/13/BookTalk%20K2/01BookTalkK2.ngsversion.1450125001044.adapt.1900.1.jpg">

    </div>

    <div class="md:p-2 p-1 w--1/2"><!--width and parameters are set here for the images-->

    <img alt="gallery" class="w-full object-cover h-full object-center block" src="https://i.pinimg.com/564x/b7/6d/5f/b76d5fd35e22be4691ea6cd01f333520.jpg">

    </div>

    <div class="md:p-2 p-1 w--1/2">

    <img alt="gallery" class="w-full object-cover h-full object-center block" src="https://i.pinimg.com/564x/55/53/ee/5553ee13b20e7a6f74599afa1e7d5bd8.jpg">

</section><hr>

<section class="text-gray-700 body-font"><!--this section displays quotes on the page-->

 <div class="container px-5 py-24 mx--auto">
```

```html
    <div class="xl:w-1/2 lg:w-3/4 w-full mx-auto text-center"><!--
text allignment is set here-->

      <svg xmlns="http://www.w3.org/2000/svg" fill="currentColor"
class="inline-block w-8 h-8 text-gray-400 mb-
8" viewBox="0 0 975.036 975.036">

        <path d="M925.036 57.197h-304c-27.6 0-50 22.4-
50 50v304c0 27.601 22.4 50 50 50h145.5c-1.9 79.601-20.4 143.3-
55.4 191.2-27.6 37.8-69.399 69.1-125.3 93.8-25.7 11.3-36.8 41.7-
24.8 67.101l36 76c11.6 24.399 40.3 35.1 65.1 24.399 66.2-
28.6 122.101-64.8 167.7-108.8 55.601-53.7 93.7-114.3 114.3-
181.9 20.601-67.6 30.9-159.8 30.9-276.8v-239c0-27.599-22.401-50-
50-50zM106.036 913.497c65.4-28.5 121-64.699 166.9-108.6 56.1-
53.7 94.4-114.1 115-181.2 20.6-67.1 30.899-159.6 30.899-277.5v-
239c0-27.6-22.399-50-50-50h-304c-27.6 0-50 22.4-
50 50v304c0 27.601 22.4 50 50 50h145.5c-1.9 79.601-20.4 143.3-
55.4 191.2-27.6 37.8-69.4 69.1-125.3 93.8-25.7 11.3-36.8 41.7-
24.8 67.101l35.9 75.8c11.601 24.399 40.501 35.2 65.301 24.399z"><
/path>

      </svg><!--
this is the quote entity taken from an external source-->
```

```html
    <p class="leading-relaxed text-lg">There are no foreign lands. It is the traveller only who is foreign. </p><br>

    <h2 class="text-gray-900 font-medium title-font tracking-wider text-sm">Robert Louis Stevenson</h2>

    <p class="text-gray-500">(1850–1894)</p><br><hr><br><!--space and horizontal rule is added to the text-->

    <p class="leading-relaxed text-lg">May the road rise up to meet you.<br>May the wind be always at your back.<br>May the sun shine warm upon your face;<br>The rains fall soft upon your fields.<br>And until we meet again,<br>May God hold you in the palm of His hand.</p><!--here br adds line breaks-->

    <br>

    <h2 class="text-gray-900 font-medium title-font tracking-wider text-sm">Anonymous</h2>

  </div>

 </div>

</section><hr>

 <section class="text-gray-700 body-font light-bg relative"><!--this section embeds a youtube video in the page-->
```

```html
<br>

<br>

<div class="container px-100 py-200 mx-auto">

    <div class="xl:w-1/2 lg:w-3/4 w-full mx-auto text-center">

    <h1 class="sm:text-3xl text-2xl font-medium title-font mb-2 text-gray-900 tracking-widest mb-1">THE BEAUTY OF PAKISTAN </h1><!--text is added before the video-->

    <br>

    <br>

</div>

    <center><iframe width="1280" height="720" src="https://www.youtube.com/embed/XZ1NcwErw2s"></iframe></center> <!--the video is centre aligned by using user-defined tags and placing the link in iframe tag-->

    </section><br><br><br><hr><!--also the height and width have been set-->

  <section class="text-gray-700 body-font relative"><!--this section gives us an embeded map along with a form on top-->
```

```html
<div class="absolute inset-0 bg-gray-300">

    <iframe width="100%" height="100%" frameborder="0" margi
nheight="0" marginwidth="0" title="map" scrolling="no" src="https:
//www.google.com/maps/embed?pb=!1m18!1m12!1m3!1d705
5507.901124105!2d64.85647039457444!3d30.29200565752809
4!2m3!1f0!2f0!3f0!3m2!1i1024!2i768!4f13.1!3m3!1m2!1s0x38db52d2f8f
d751f%3A0x46b7a1f7e614925c!2sPakistan!5e0!3m2!1sen!2s!4v16
08027816971!5m2!1sen!2s"></iframe>

  </div><!--
using iframe the borders and height width have been set for the
 map-->

  <div class="container px-5 py-24 mx-auto flex"><!--
this section has form for adding feedback-->

    <div class="lg:w-1/3 md:w-1/2 bg-white rounded-lg p-
8 flex flex-col md:ml-auto w-full mt-10 md:mt-0 relative z-10">

      <form action="/form-action.html" method="get"><!--
using form attribute feedback is added here-->

      <h2 class="text-gray-900 text-lg mb-1 font-medium title-
font">Feedback</h2>

      <p class="leading-relaxed mb-5 text-gray-
600">Let us know what you think of our website.</p>
```

```html
    <div class="relative mb-4">

        <label for="email" class="leading-7 text-sm text-gray-600">Email</label>

        <input type="email" id="email" name="email" class="w-full bg-white rounded border border-gray-300 focus:border-green-500 text-base outline-none text-gray-700 py-1 px-3 leading-8 transition-colors duration-200 ease-in-out">

    </div>

    <div class="relative mb-4"><!--message can be added in this part of the form-->

        <label for="message" class="leading-7 text-sm text-gray-600">Message</label>

        <textarea id="message" name="message" class="w-full bg-white rounded border border-gray-300 focus:border-green-500 h-32 text-base outline-none text-gray-700 py-1 px-3 resize-none leading-6 transition-colors duration-200 ease-in-out"></textarea>

    </div>

    <button class="text-white bg-green-500 border-0 py-2 px-6 focus:outline-none hover:bg-green-600 rounded text-lg">
```

```html
    <a href="form-action.html">Submit</a></button><!--
a button is created that directs the user to a page where a conf
irmation message is displayed-->

    <p class="text-xs text-gray-500 mt-
3">Covering all parts of Pakistan</p>

  </form>

  </div>

 </div>

</section><br><br><br><hr>

<footer class="text-gray-700 body-font"><!--
the footer of the page is defined here-->

  <div class="container px-5 py-24 mx-auto flex md:items-
center lg:items-start md:flex-row md:flex-no-wrap flex-wrap flex-
col">

    <div class="w-64 flex-shrink-0 md:mx-0 mx-auto text-
center md:text-left"><!--
setting the borders and allignment of footers-->

    <a class="flex title-font font-medium items-center md:justify-
start justify-center text-gray-900">
```

```html
        <img width="120px" height="100px" src="images\logo.jpg"
><!--
an image for the logo is added here using img tag nad setting it
s height width-->
        <span class="ml-3 text-xl text-500 tracking-
widest">Trip Companion</span>
    </a><br><hr>
    <p class="mt-2 text-sm text-gray-
500">Where great journeys begin.</p>
    </div>
    <div class="flex-grow flex flex-wrap md:pl-20 -mb-10 md:mt-
0 mt-10 md:text-left text-center"><!--
subheadings are made to divide the footers of the page-->
    <div class="lg:w-1/4 md:w-1/2 w-full px-4">
    <h2 class="title-font font-medium text-gray-900 tracking-
widest text-sm mb-3">HOME</h2><hr><br>
    <nav class="list-none mb-10">
    <li>
```

```html
        <a class="text-gray-600 hover:text-gray-
800" href="main.html">Home</a><!--
each text is linked using href with the page it states-->

      </li>

      <li>

        <a class="text-gray-600 hover:text-gray-
800" href="BLOG.HTML">Blogs</a>

      </li>

      <li>

        <a class="text-gray-600 hover:text-gray-
800" href="takeyourtrip.html">Trips</a>

      </li>

      <li>

        <a class="text-gray-600 hover:text-gray-
800" href="aboutus.html">About Us</a>

      </li>

    </nav>

  </div>

    <div class="lg:w-1/4 md:w-1/2 w-full px-4"><!--
another sub list of footers is added here-->
```

```html
<h2 class="title-font font-medium text-gray-900 tracking-widest text-sm mb-3">EXPLORE</h2><hr><br>

    <nav class="list-none mb-10">

    <li><!--the li tag is used to make list-->

      <a class="text-gray-600 hover:text-gray-800" href="Punjab.html">Punjab</a>

    </li>

    <li>

      <a class="text-gray-600 hover:text-gray-800" href="Sindh.html">Sindh</a>

    </li>

    <li>

      <a class="text-gray-600 hover:text-gray-800" href="Balochistan.html">Balochistan</a>

    </li>

    <li>

      <a class="text-gray-600 hover:text-gray-800" href="Khyber Pakhtunkhwa.html">Khyber Pakhtunkhwa</a>

    </li>

    <li>
```

```html
            <a class="text-gray-600 hover:text-gray-
800" href="Kashmir.html">Kashmir</a>

        </li>

      </nav>

    </div>

    <div class="lg:w-1/4 md:w-1/2 w-full px-4">

      <h2 class="title-font font-medium text-gray-900 tracking-
widest text-sm mb-3">CITIES</h2><hr><br>

      <nav class="list-none mb-10">

        <li>

          <a class="text-gray-600 hover:text-gray-
800" href="Islamabad.html">Islamabad</a>

        </li>

        <li>

          <a class="text-gray-600 hover:text-gray-
800" href="Lahore.html">Lahore</a>

        </li>

        <li>

          <a class="text-gray-600 hover:text-gray-
800" href="Karachi.html">Karachi</a>
```

```html
    </li>

    <li>

    <a class="text-gray-600 hover:text-gray-
800" href="Peshawer.html">Peshawer</a>

    </li>

    <li>

    <a class="text-gray-600 hover:text-gray-
800" href="Murree.html">Murree</a>

    </li>

    </nav>

    </div>

    <div class="lg:w-1/4 md:w-1/2 w-full px-4"><!--
a total of 4 sub lists are made in the footer using the same techi
que as above-->

    <h2 class="title-font font-medium text-gray-900 tracking-
widest text-sm mb-3">CITIES</h2><hr><br>

    <nav class="list-none mb-10">

    <li>

    <a class="text-gray-600 hover:text-gray-
800" href="Hunza.html">Hunza</a>
```

```html
    </li>

    <li>

      <a class="text-gray-600 hover:text-gray-
800" href="Skardu.html">Skardu</a>

    </li>

    <li>

      <a class="text-gray-600 hover:text-gray-
800" href="Swat.html">Swat Valley</a>

    </li>

    <li>

      <a class="text-gray-600 hover:text-gray-
800" href="Quetta.html">Quetta</a>

    </li>

    <li>

      <a class="text-gray-600 hover:text-gray-
800" href="Rawalpindi.html">Rawalpindi</a>

    </li>

    </nav>

    </div>
```

```
    </div>

    </div>

  </footer>

</body><!--here the body of the page ends-->

</html><!--the page code ends here with the html tag-->
```

Note: Links to the unavailable images can be changed to run the webpage smoothly. Here is how the webpage will look on the server.

BLOGS

Inspiration for your next trip!

Blog Post

10 Must Visit Places in Islamabad

Islamabad is a beautiful, clean and lush green capital of Pakistan. It is no wonder it is considered the 2nd most beautiful capital in the world.

Read More →

👁 1.2K   🗨 4

Blog Post

Pakistan through the eyes of travelers

It was another visa run visit to Pakistan. My second one this year so far. It was a short trip, long enough to be bored at home doing nothing but too short to explore Pakistan like I did in the previous visit.

Read More →

👁 1.2K   🗨 4

Blog Post

Planning your trip to Snow in Pakistan

If you are planning a trip to the snowy mountains. Choosing the best travel guide would be your first priority. The popular resorts of Malam Jabba and Naltar Valley offer skiing and snowboarding for all abilities.

Read More →

👁 1.2K   🗨 6

" "

There are no foreign lands. It is the traveller only who is foreign.

Robert Louis Stevenson
(1850-1894)

May the road rise up to meet you.
May the wind be always at your back.
May the sun shine warm upon your face;
The rains fall soft upon your fields.
And until we meet again,
May God hold you in the palm of His hand.

Anonymous

THE BEAUTY OF PAKISTAN

Trip Companion

Where great journeys begin.

HOME	EXPLORE	CITIES	CITIES
Home	Punjab	Islamabad	Hunza
Blogs	Sindh	Lahore	Skardu
Trips	Balochistan	Karachi	Swat Valley
About Us	Khyber Pakhtunkhwa	Peshawar	Quetta
	Kashmir	Murree	Rawalpindi

Chapter 5: Mistakes to avoid in HTML

5.1: Basic Syntax and Implementation Errors

The list consists of often created HTML markup errors by front-end web developers. If you are a first-time a programmer or web designer interested in experimenting with UI architecture, try to prevent these errors.

Missing DOCTYPE:

To begin, DOCTYPE displays your current HTML version to various browsers. You can't be sure the coding is correct without it. When a DOCTYPE is missing, the browser begins to make conclusions. In this scenario, the outcome of your efforts could not be as lucrative as you had hoped.

To stop it, take the following advice:

- No matter what kind of HTML you have, use DOCTYPE.

- It should always be the first line of the code root.

- Keep in mind that the DOCTYPE is case-sensitive.

- Create an empty doc template save your DOCTYPE so you can use it quickly.

- To find potential openings, use HTML verifiers and CSS tools.

Wrong HTML blocks placement:

This standard HTML website design error of judgment also has an organizational component. To summarize, an HTML element is shown as Block or Inline by default. Therein lies the problem that we live in the era of intelligent technology; many users also put block elements contained by inline elements.

Wrong: <a href="#"><h2>This is a block within Inline</h2></a>

Right: <h2><a href="#">This is inline within Block</a></h2>

To stop making this error, keep in mind the following:

- The layout of your text is defined by block elements, such as paragraphs or divs
- Inline elements, such as tags and anchors, are considered blocks.

Although inline elements are contained inside blocks, they are not identical. Never have blocks inside inline modules.

Missing close tags:

So, here is another typical HTML problem. Although some beginners skip any of the fundamental tags, others overlook the near ones, such as:

<div>	</div>
<head>	</head>
<body>	</body>

Messy CSS Organization:

One of the most frequent errors users create when writing CSS is insufficient structuring. They place a greater emphasis on content and graphic aspects of websites than on logically organizing types. Typically, novices write their CSS in the order in which they think about them. As a result, users cannot locate a style declaration until the time comes to update it. It suggests that you arrange CSS under the organization of the HTML on which you work. For instance:

- Header

- Body

- Sidebar

- Footer

Missing alt tag:

For IMG tags, the ALT attribute is required; it specifies the image's meaning. It assists your user who is using screen readers or has a slow link in determining the importance of the picture. Additionally, it improves the web crawler's indexing of the subjects. If the images are purely decorative, using empty ALT attributes such as alt=" ".

Wrong: <img src="picture.jpeg"/>

Right: <img src=" picture.jpeg" alt="Picture "/>

Don't remove border attribute:

The border is a presentational feature that should be semantically changed in CSS instead of the HTML script.

Wrong: <img src="picture.png" border="0"/>

Right: <img src="picture.jpg"/>

Avoid deprecated elements:

Few older HTML attributes and tags have been designated as deprecated by the W3C consortium. While existing browsers support them, they may not be in the future.

Code tables carefully:

It is better to skip table tags and only use organized <divs>. It is to call attention to tables as one of the most frequent causes of incorrect HTML. People believe the browsers are unconcerned about everything. However, improperly coded tables can destroy your credibility when it comes to assistive technology.

Using Wrong HTML extensions:

To conclude, let us discuss the famous HTML extension align=absmiddle. Yes, it is widely used in the world. Nonetheless, this does not make the Attribute universally applicable. Take note that align=absmiddle is not sufficient to generate proper HTML for the picture tag.

Error: <img src = "image.gif" align = "absmiddle">

However, it should be corrected! Since many browsers support the extension, it causes your HTML to become wrong. It is suggested that you must use align=middle.

Conclusion

Congratulations on your achievement! You have now created your very own page. You also studied the architecture facets of web creation and how to program in HTML. When it comes to creating a website, you can learn what works and what does not by reviewing various websites.

Anyone, who will learn a foreign language, will learn to code. Programming is like speaking a foreign language, which is why it is called programming languages. Each has its own set of rules and syntax that must be mastered in order. Those laws are instructions for your machine. They are ways of showing the browsers what to do in web programming, more precisely.

Regardless of the size of a platform or the amount of technology involved, HTML is at the center of any web page. It is a must-have talent for those working in the online industry. It is a great place to start if you're interested in learning how to make web material. And, fortunately for us, it is effortless to pick up.

This book will learn the basic concepts of HTML and how to implement them on primary web pages. All the codes used in this book have been explained along with their syntax. Keeping in mind that this book is a beginner's guide to learning how to code

HTML, some of the concepts have not been added to avoid confusion while learning.

It is advised that HTML, CSS, and JavaScript should also be learned to build more interactive front-end websites and user interfaces.